Heal With Me
&
Our Journey Goes On

Written & Illustrated
by Ali Marsman

 **Friesen Press**

Suite 300 - 990 Fort St
Victoria, BC, Canada, V8V 3K2
www.friesenpress.com

ISBN
978-1-4602-6064-7 (Paperback)
978-1-4602-6065-4 (eBook)

1. Poetry

Distributed to the trade by The Ingram Book Company

I welcome your comments. Please let me know what you think by writing to me at **alimarsman@alms-houseproducts.com** and placing '**Comments**' in the subject line.

For information about permission to reproduce selections from this book, for reasons other than personal reference and growth, please write with '**Permission**' in the subject line.

For a schedule of upcoming workshops and seminars, or if you are interested in bringing one to your area, please place, '**Workshops and Seminars**' in the subject line, or click on the calendar.

I welcome your comments, thoughts, and questions about other ALM's House Products; (bookmarks, calendars, cards, music, and posters) please write to me with '**Products**' in the subject line, or visit the website and click on products and services.

ALMsHouseProducts.com

Dear Holly,

I am so happy to have met you...
a fellow author! I wish you the
greatest success in life and hope
you continue to write into old age!

Sincerely,
Ali Marsman (a friend!)

©19

Thank You for acquiring a copy of my poetry book. If this finds you at a difficult time in your life; I hope you are able to find at least one poem that helps you to feel better. Feel free to write it out, and carry it with you for whenever you need help with your healing.

Chin up, Up, UP!

Sincerely,
Ali

Table of Contents

Heal With Me

I'm letting go. I'm breaking free
of all this sorrow inside of me.
The pain is leaving. It's going away;
I am tired of these unhappy days.
I'm moving on without this pain;
I am tired of feeling so drained.
I'm letting go. I'm breaking free
of all this sorrow inside of me.
I'm going on to a fresh new start;
I have lived too long with this broken heart.
I'm letting go. I will be free;
come on everybody...Heal With Me!

&

Our Journey Goes On

Heal With Me, and
Our Journey Goes On...
we're healing together,
to change what's wrong;
we're learning to believe,
and love ourselves;
we're learning to contend,
so that all is well;
you're healing yourself,
while I heal me;
we'll become even stronger,
now that we've begun this journey!

4" x 6" photo

Believe In Yourself!

I am beautiful!
I will no longer believe you as I have before.
I am deserving!
What you said does not matter to me anymore.
I am strong!
You will no longer bring me down.
I will heal!
Because of the greatness in me that I have found.
I will succeed!
At what I want that is best for me.
I am elated!
Because of all the fine things in me I see.
I am outstanding!
It shows in everything that I have done.
I do believe!
In myself, which means I have won.
I am intelligent!
Because of what I now believe.
I am wonderful!
It does not matter any longer what you see.
I am lovable!
I do not need to hear this from you.
My feelings count!
Along with all the things that I have been through.
I am beautiful. I am elated. **I am intelligent.**
I am deserving. **I am lovable.** I am wonderful.
I will succeed. I am outstanding. **I do believe.**
My feelings count, **and** I am strong!
All the negative things I allowed into my head
were so very, very wrong!

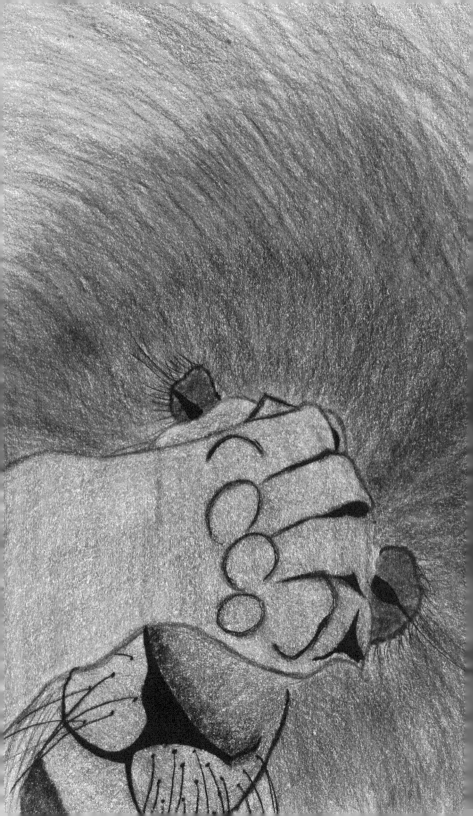

The Courage?

Do I have the courage to heal?
Will I be able to fight?
Do I have what it takes to heal?
Will I try with all my might?
Do I have the valour to cure?
Will I handle this fray?
Will I be able to endure it
until victory day?
Do I have fearlessness to heal,
so I'll no longer cry?
Will I get past the fact
that I want to die?
Do I have the power to restore,
so I can start to smile?
Will I hang in there? Will I be brave?
Even if it takes a while?
Do I have the strength to battle
the thoughts that formed so young?
Will I stay, and tough it out
until the day I've won?
Do I have the potency to last?
Will I stay with you?
Will I do whatever it takes?
Well, I sure hope I do!

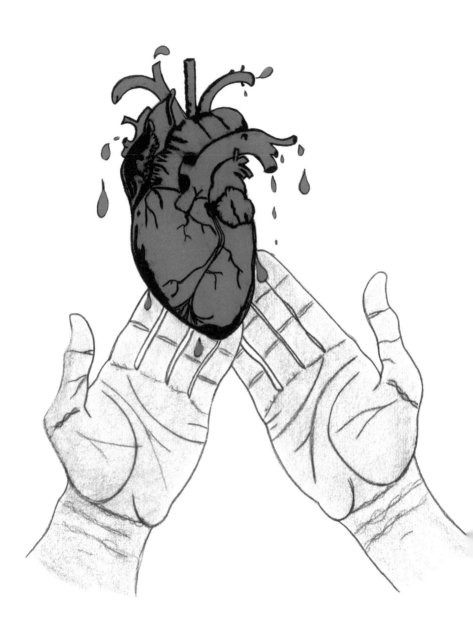

You Say...

You say you are happy,
but there's pain in your eyes;
You speak so joyous constantly,
but I know you want to cry;
You seem to look deep in my eyes,
but I know you're looking through;
You say you are happy,
but I know that's not the truth.
You say we are friends,
but I can see our ties are severing;
I try to hold your hand,
but you won't get close, ever;
You seem to want to pour your heart,
it's something that's good to do;
You say that you are fine,
please tell me...is this true?
You say you are rested,
but you always gape;
You try to be on time,
but you're always late;
Why don't you just let it all out?
You can pour your heart out to me...
You say that nothing is wrong with you,
but that's not what I see.

There's No Hope

I can't heal,
there's too much pain.
There's no hope,
I'm drowning in rain.
I'm all alone,
there's nobody around.
It's too difficult,
I can only frown.
I'm damaged badly,
I can't go on.
I'm not okay,
what happened was wrong.
It's not worth it,
my heart won't mend.
It's my fault,
from beginning to end.
I'm nobody special.
I won't be missed.

There Is Hope!

I can heal,
the pain will subside!
There is hope,
you are by my side!
I am not alone,
I do have friends!
It is hard,
but I will be strong to the end!
I am damaged,
but not forever!
I'll be just fine,
because I am clever!
It is worth it,
I have so much to give!
It is not my fault,
it is something they did.
I am special!
I would be missed!

As Long As

As long as I am laughing,
I don't have to cry;
as long as I am smiling,
you won't ask me why.
As long as I am busy,
you won't notice me;
as long as I am occupied,
my pain you won't see.
As long as I am drunk,
I won't have any fears;
as long as I am rummy,
I won't have any care.
As long as I am high,
I don't have to reflect;
as long as I am stoned,
I don't have to protect.
As long as I am running,
I can leave my mind;
as long as I am exerting,
I'll leave bad memories behind.
As long as I am lying,
I will never heal;
as long as I am deluded,
my abuse is no big deal.

Confusion

The courage to heal,
for the fear I'll founder?
The fearlessness to confide,
for the fault you'll ponder?
The desire to better,
for the vigour I shall find?
The wanting to confer,
but hesitation in mind?
The hindrance to laugh,
the anguish to cry?
The bother to exist,
for I am too strong to die!

I can take, Or I Can Deal!

I can take that much hurt,
and be that sad,
thinking of the life that I wanted to have ...
I can feel this much pain,
and be this depressed,
because of all of the things I have tried to repress ...
I can take that much damage,
and be this glum,
constantly blaming myself for what's been done ...
I can take this much harm,
and be this dejected,
constantly racking my brain as to why I feel rejected ...
Or
I can deal with the hurt,
and feel pain once in a while ...
I can be happy sometimes,
and I can even laugh and smile ...
I can realize I was damaged,
because I know I was wronged ...
finally; then I will believe my worthiness,
and just move on.

It's Hard To Look Hopeful

I cannot 'un-remember,'
I've remembered for years;
I only know how to hurt,
and how to live in fear.
I cannot 'un-recall,'
I've tried to stabilize my mind;
I can only see the pain,
happiness I cannot find.
I cannot 'un-retain,'
pain is all I know;
it's so unnatural not to cry,
so I simply let go.
I cannot 'un-remind,'
everything looks so low;
it's really hard to smile,
when all you feel is woe.
I cannot 'un-reminisce,'
they are the only memories I see;
unless, I make up something wonderful,
where I could include me.
I cannot 'un-remember,'
I've remembered too long;
it's hard to look hopeful,
when life feels so wrong.

It Can Be Hopeful!

I may not 'un-remember,'
but I can certainly deal;
I can do whatever it takes,
so I can finally heal.
I may not 'un-recall,'
but I can stabilize my mind;
I can surely cope with things,
so happiness I will find.
I may not 'un-retain,'
but I can certainly try,
so that I care not to
ask the question: 'why?'
I may not 'un-remind,'
but I can start to move on;
I can stop blaming myself,
and believing I am wrong.
I may not 'un-reminisce,'
but I can create new memories,
so when I look back on my life;
wonderful memories I will see.
I may not 'un-remember,'
but I will certainly deal;
I will do whatever it takes,
so I can say, 'I am healed!'

Beautiful Flowers

Just watch how the beautiful flowers,
keep their petals all in place;
they are not growing up too fast,
but at a steady pace;
the glow that comes off these flowers,
twinkles like a star;
because they all are standing tall,
so proud of who they are.

We are all beautiful flowers,
living in this world;
look at all the beautiful men and women ...
all the beautiful boys and girls.
We all need to stand really tall,
and be proud of who we are;
then we will see a glow from us,
that shines just like a star!

Only I Can Know

I love it when it's raining,
I love to see the rain;
it's such an easy thing to use
to cover up my pain.
When the rain is pouring down my face,
it's hard to see the tears;
there is no way anyone can tell
just how much sorrow is here.
I love it when it's raining;
I love to see it pour,
because my tears I won't hold back
like when the sun shines outdoors.
I love it when it pours so hard
it is impossible to see,
because I know that nobody
can truly see me.
I love it when it's raining,
I hope for rain each day;
I'd have it raining all day and night
if I had things my way.
I love it when it's grey outside,
that means it's going to rain;
I don't much like seeing the sun,
it can't cover up my pain.
If I get caught in the rain,
and the sun starts to show;
please don't ask me why I cry,
only I can know.

I Will Help You

I don't like to see the rain,
I know you're going to cry;
I know the rain is an easy thing
when tears you want to hide.
When the rain is pouring down your face,
I can see your tears;
I will be here to help you through,
and hold you very near.
I don't like it when it's raining;
I don't like when it pours,
because I cannot watch you cry
the way I have before.
I don't like when it pours so hard
it is impossible to see,
because I want to see your pain,
so I can help thee.
I don't like it when it's raining,
you don't have to hide your tears;
I will be here right by your side
to help you with your fears.
I will help you to have clear skies,
no need for them to be grey;
I want to help you find happiness ...
if I may?
If you get caught in the rain,
and the sun starts to show;
that's when I will take your hand,
and never let it go.

Hurting Children

Why did Billy, a nine year old,
burn his house down?
And on his face, he never smiles,
you only see a frown?
Why did Sarah, an eleven year old,
run away from home?
She had no one to run to,
she ran all alone.
These children are not trouble makers,
they really hurt within;
they want their lives to be bright,
but right now it is dim.
Please don't blame these children,
for someone has hurt them really badly,
because if you look deep within their eyes
you will see, they are really sad.
Give these children lots of time;
show them that you care,
and if you feel the need to;
shed with them their tears.
We need to show these children,
that things can, and will be okay;
we need to listen closely,
to what they have to say.
We must stop the bad things
that go unheard;
before Sarah disappears for good,
and another house Billy burns.

'native to all of us'

Little Boy? Part One

"Little boy, why are you sad?
Why so much pain there in your eyes?
Little boy, why don't you talk?
Why so many deep, deep sighs?
Little boy, why are you all alone?
Why is there no one in whom you confide?
Little boy, why no support for you?
Why isn't anyone at your side?
Little boy, why do you cry?
Why are your eyes so red?
Little boy, why all the sorrow?
Why do you wish you were dead?
Little boy, why do you stumble?
Why so many needle-pricks and holes?
Little boy, why are you always drunk?
Why doesn't anybody know?
Little boy, why don't you come home?
Why don't you come home with me?
Little boy, things will get better?
Why don't you come home and see?"

'native to all of us'

Little Girl? Part One

"Little girl, why are you sad?
Why so much pain there in your eyes?
Little girl, why don't you talk?
Why so many deep, deep sighs?
Little girl, why are you all alone?
Why is there no one in whom you confide?
Little girl, why no support for you?
Why isn't anyone at your side?
Little girl, why do you cry?
Why are your eyes so red?
Little girl, why all the sorrow?
Why do you wish you were dead?
Little girl, why do you stumble?
Why so many needle-pricks and holes?
Little girl, why are you always drunk?
Why doesn't anybody know?
Little girl, why don't you come home?
Why don't you come home with me?
Little girl, things will get better?
Why don't you come home and see?"

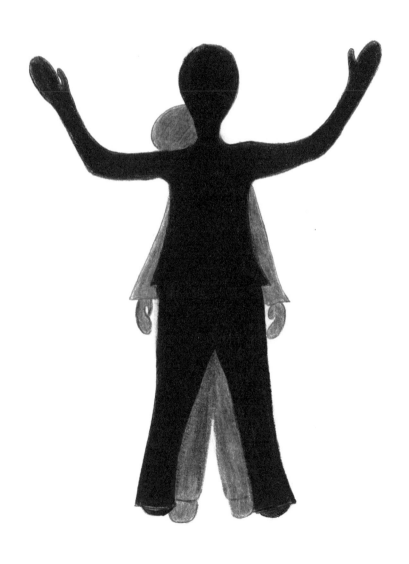

{ Ali Marsman

Please!

Please give me a hug,
even though I say 'no.'
Please hold my hand tight,
and don't let go.
Will you help flip my frown around?
I'm counting on you,
please don't let me down.
Please talk to me,
when I seem blue;
even if
I won't say a word to you.
Please do all of the talking,
until I can;
please help me up,
so I can stand.

Please... give me a hug!

Because You Want To

Smile because you want to,
not because you must;
laugh when you need to,
let it be your instincts you trust;
cry when you ought to,
when you're feeling low;
be silly when you'd like to,
when you want to let go.

Lend a hand when you desire,
not when you feel obliged;
give a hug when it's necessary,
when your arms are open wide;
express your feelings, it's essential;
show your feelings when you can...
express yourself entirely;
while considering how you do it, and when.

How Long?

How long does it hurt?
How long does pain last?
When will I stop feeling,
these feelings from my past?
When will the nightmares end?
How long do they stay?
Are they here forever?
Will they always end my days?
When can I stop pretending?
When will I cry?
Will I take a normal breath,
instead of sigh after sigh?
When will I break the shell,
I've been living in?
When will my days,
no longer be dark and dim?
When will I love myself?
Will I ever care?
When will these destructive thoughts,
be far away from here?
When will I start to live?
Will I always only exist?
Will I ever be recognized?
For me they always miss.
How long does it hurt?
Just how long does pain last?
When will I stop feeling,
those feelings from the past?

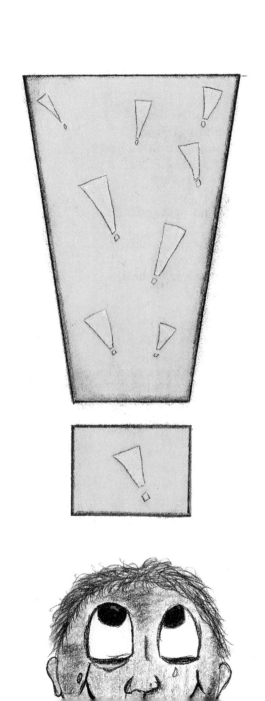

Pain Does End!

It will not hurt forever,
the pain does end!
The nightmares will go away,
once your feelings mend!
There is no need to pretend,
if you need to, Cry!
Take nice deep breaths,
for there's no need to sigh!
Start chipping away your shell,
so you can see the light!
You must believe you are worth it,
that's the beginning of your fight!
You've done wonderfully thus far,
your courage has always existed!
As long as you believe your worthiness,
it doesn't matter who else sees it!
It will not hurt forever!
The pain does end!
Hold your chin up really high,
and you'll do just fine, my friend!

Feelings?

Feelings?
What feelings?
Just look at my face ...
I'm completely numb,
my feelings are erased.
How do you feel pleasure?
How are you satisfied?
How do you feel sadness,
when someone has died?
How do you feel angry,
when someone has deceived you?
How do you get excited?
What is feeling blue?
How do you get frustrated,
when you can't complete a chore?
How exactly do you laugh,
until you can't anymore?
How do you feel frightened,
when someone gives you a scare?
How do you show appreciation,
when someone truly cares?
How do you feel proud,
when you've done something great?
How do you show (un)conditional love?
Is there such a feeling as hate?
How do you show confusion,
when something blows your mind?
How do you feel lonely,
when you are left behind?
What is feeling happy?
How is it when you're glad?
Feelings?
What are feelings?
Are they something I will have?

Tears Of A Clown

Only the actions of a clown,
can hide so much misery.
Only that much make-up disguises,
what you don't want anyone to see.
Only such baggy clothing,
covers up your dealings.
Only the constant telling of jokes,
camouflages your feelings.
Only when acting like a clown,
you can quiet your tears.
You make people laugh so hard,
they simple cannot hear.
Only when acting like a clown,
you can conceal your woe?
Only the tears of a clown
can hide your grief...does anyone know?

The Key To Your Happiness

You hung in there
through the sleepless nights;
through all of the loneliness,
and battles you had to fight;
you continue to hold on
to the strength that is you;
no need to quit now ...
keep doing as you do.

You endured all the criticism,
and dealt with the pain;
you continued to see sunshine
through the pouring rain;
you resisted all the negative words
through the hardest times;
you pursued the belief in you,
so contentment you would find ...

You remain proud of yourself,
for it has been a long, long road;
the key to your happiness
only you can hold.

Why I'm Holding On

This pain that I feel,
is definitely strong;
that's why I don't understand,
why I'm holding on.
Wouldn't it be easier,
just letting it go?
Or should I stay with this pain,
and get use to feeling low?
This pain that I feel,
is definitely strong;
that's why I understand,
why I no longer must hold on.

You're The One!

You're in charge of your life,
and how much happiness there will be;
you're in control of your pain,
and how much you'll let others see;
you're the one who guides the sadness,
in how much you'll endure;
you're the one who has the power,
I know those things for sure.

You're in charge of your life,
and how successful you'll become;
you're in control of a fortunate future,
that needs to be won;
you're in charge of your intelligence,
in how much information you know;
you're the one with the capacity,
of helping your mind grow.

Only you have the influence.
It is yourself you must promote.
Once you take charge of you;
I tell you, there is hope!

A Hope For Healing

There's a hope for healing ...
an expectation to cure;
there's faith to repair,
those feelings from before;
there's confidence to rebuild ...
an anticipation to mend;
there's a desire to help,
because you are my friend!

Reclaim Yourself

It's time to reclaim your life,
the carelessness you knew;
the easygoing, merry person,
who once was you.

Let's get back those smiles,
you gave each day,
and rescue your optimism ...
the positive things you'd say.

Let's take away your sorrow,
and get rid of your despair;
let's leave depression far behind,
and dry up all those tears.

Start worrying about yourself ...
the wonderful person you are;
leave your beauty as it is,
and let's not cause no more harm.

It's time to reclaim your life,
the carelessness you knew;
that wonderful, outstanding, intelligent person ...
that beautiful, gifted, inspiring person ...
who is inside of you!

My Entire Self ... I Believe In Me!

I believe in myself,
and in everything I do;
in my distinguishing characteristics,
and in everything I do!
I fancy my intelligence,
and, as well, my intellect;
how easily I remember things,
and even when I forget;
I trust my instincts,
as a safety builder;
in its foreshadowing techniques,
and ways it bewilders;
I hold my morals closely,
and do what's best for me;
I always remember first,
what I value and believe;
I support my achievements,
in their entirety;
in how they make me feel content,
and all filled up with glee;
I credit myself greatly,
for toughing life out;
for hanging in there strongly,
even when consumed with doubt;
I finally accept myself,
and everything that is me;
my mind, my body, and spiritual self...
my entire self ... I believe in me!

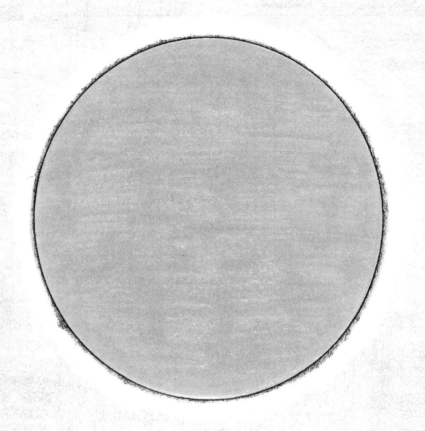

You Should Not; You Should!

You should not
be in the dark;
You should
see the light;
You should not
give up on life;
You should
definitely fight.

You should not
be sad;
You should
certainly smile.
You should
believe all is possible,
or
You should learn how!

What Do You Mean To You?

What do you mean to you?
What do you really mean?
Are you worth an incredible future?
Are you worth fulfilling your dreams?
Do you deserve to be happy?
Do you deserve to smile?
Are you worth sharing your views,
and being right, without being denied?

What do you mean to you?
What do you really mean?
Do you deserve to be with others ...
to be placed within a team?
Do you deserve more than what you have?
I think you know you do!
But first believe what you mean;
what you really mean to you!

My Happiness!

From this moment,
there's a new me;
only wonderful things,
you will see.

I am no longer a victim,
I have survived;
there's no more cheerlessness,
I feel alive.

I walk with a smile,
and my head up high;
I sing to myself,
there are no more sighs.

I hop along the streets,
I enjoy the outdoors;
there are so many pleasures,
I have yet to endure.

I live for the moment,
I enjoy each and every day;
I can't believe the happiness,
and it's here to stay!

Your Life

This is about you,
and what you have endured;
it is about the happiness,
that is in store.

It deals with the hurt,
and talks about fears;
it laughs with smiles,
and cries with tears.

It skips in the rain,
and sings in the sun;
it's everything about you,
and all the great things you've done.

This is your life,
and it's all about you;
it deals with all aspects,
and everything who makes you, you!

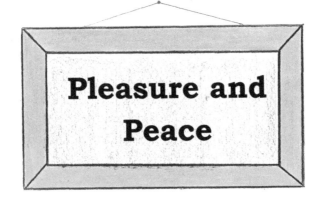

I Am Worth It!

I am worth so much more,
than what I go through;
worth more than these tears,
always feeling blue.
I deserve more than sleepless nights,
and more than exhausting days;
I deserve more than being depressed,
I am ready to change these ways ...
I have the right to innocence,
I will outgrow this pain;
I deserve to live with contentment,
instead of dread over, and again.
I will have a wonderful future,
when I remember me;
I will learn to trust others,
even if only a select few.
I will soon believe all is possible;
I will hold my head up high,
and while thinking of who I am;
I will have every reason to smile.
I am worth so much more,
than what I lived, and seen;
Contentment, **Happiness**,
Pleasure and **Peace**;
is in store for me!

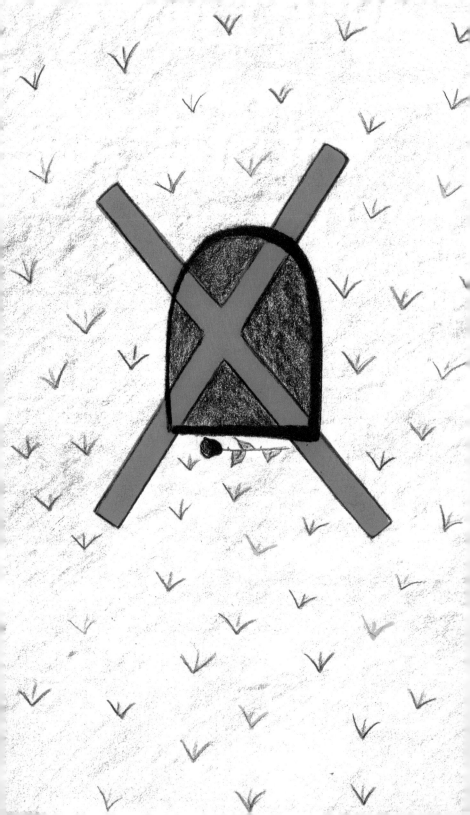

No Reason

I would really hate to lose you.
I don't want to say goodbye.
There is absolutely no reason
that you need to die.

There is so much that you've done,
and so much more for you to do;
that would make you want to live
if you only knew.

I would truly hate to free you.
I don't want to say so long.
Don't let them do this to you
they are the ones who are wrong.

I know you're in a lot of pain.
I know you've struggled for years.
I know feeling alone as you do
would cause anyone to have fears.

I would honestly hate to lose you.
I don't want to say goodbye.
There is absolutely no good reason
that you need to die.

Triumph!

Don't try to bring me down,
or tell me I'm wrong;
don't try to make me feel worthless,
like I don't belong.

Don't comment on my looks,
what's there and not there;
don't give me your negative opinion,
because I just don't care.

Don't try to belittle me,
I believe my usefulness;
don't try to make me cry,
there's too much happiness.

Don't try to discourage me
from what I can, and cannot do,
because no matter what ...
I will triumph through!

4" x 6" Photo

Repeat After Me...

I am remarkable...
I am impressive...
I am splendid...
I am special...
I am extraordinary...
I am beautiful...
I am charming...
I am intelligent...
I am clever...
I am wise...
I am lovable...
I am delightful...

Louder!

I AM REMARKABLE...
I AM IMPRESSIVE...
I AM SPLENDID...
I AM SPECIAL...
I AM EXTRAORDINARY...
I AM BEAUTIFUL...
I AM CHARMING...
I AM INTELLIGENT...
I AM CLEVER...
I AM WISE...
I AM LOVABLE...
I AM DELIGHTFUL...

I believe these things are true...
this is me...
every bit is me!

My Pain Is Gone!

I can't believe it, Pain ...
I can't believe you're gone;
I can't believe we're not friends,
we were buddies for so long.

I can't believe I won't feel you,
that you'll no longer antagonize me;
I can't believe we decided, Pain ...
to let each other be.

I can't believe it, Pain ...
I can't believe you're gone;
I can't believe we're not friends,
we were best friends for so long.

Brighter Days

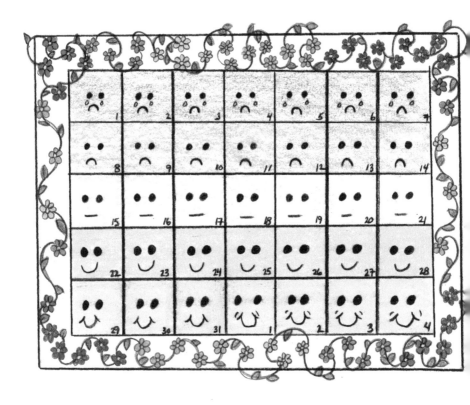

The days seem dark right now,
but soon there will be brighter days;
listen to all the positive words,
important people have to say.

Look within yourself and find,
something to make you smile;
put down this book, and think
of yourself right now ...

Think of the wonderful things,
in which you do well;
get rid of all the negative things,
and no longer on them dwell.

Look in the mirror each day,
and admire how wonderful you are;
once you start to do these things,
happiness will not be far.

Believe in yourself,
(dig deep within;)
then your days will no longer
be dark and dim.

Joey...Bright and Dark?

Joey makes others happy,
and knows just what to say;
Joey is always around,
to brighten up my days;
Joey will give anything,
and is always willing to share;
Joey always lends an ear,
and proves how much he cares...
I noticed Joey crying one day,
unlike what I am used to;
Joey is always around,
when I'm feeling blue;
does Joey have deep problems?
Ones that hurt his heart?
Joey...**happy** and **sad**?
Joey...**bright** and **dark**?
I listened closely to Joey,
and I helped him to smile;
I thought Joey had no problems,
when he was sad all the while.
I told Joey not to worry,
that I would brighten his days;
that there would be a change of help,
I'd have inspiring things to say;
now Joey, he holds his head up,
and he feels he doesn't have to put on;
Joey realizes he is important too ...
and sings to himself, happy songs.

Little Boy? Part Two

"Little boy, now that you're not sad,
and no more pain is left in your eyes ...
little boy, now that you talk,
and you breathe no more deep, deep sighs ...
little boy, now that you're not alone,
and have people in whom you confide ...
little boy, now that you have support,
and many friends right by your side ...
little boy, now that you no longer cry,
and now that your eyes are not red ...
little boy, now that you have no sorrow,
and you are glad you are not dead ...
little boy, since you no longer stumble,
and you have no new needle-pricks, or holes ...
little boy, now that you are no longer drunk,
and you want the world to know ...
little boy, are you glad you came home?
are you glad you came home with me?
Little boy, you are so much better,
and this is wonderful to see!"

Little Girl? Part Two

"Little girl, now that you're not sad,
and no more pain is left in your eyes ...
little girl, now that you talk,
and you breathe no more deep, deep sighs ...
little girl, now that you're not alone,
and have people in whom you confide ...
little girl, now that you have support,
and many friends right by your side ...
little girl, now that you no longer cry,
and now that your eyes are not red ...
little girl, now that you have no sorrow,
and you are so glad you are not dead ...
little girl, since you no longer stumble,
and you have no new needle-pricks, or holes ...
little girl, now that you are no longer drunk,
and you want the world to know ...
little girl, are you glad you came home?
are you glad you came home with me?
Little girl, you are so much better,
and this is wonderful to see!"

Your Angel

I Will Comfort You
Through The Lonely Nights;
I Will Assure That
Things Will Be Just Right;
I'll Be Beside You
When You Awaken From
A Frightful Dream;
I'll Be There, I Am You, Angel,
Here To Console Thee.
All Through These Lonely Nights
I Will Hold Your Hand;
I Will Help Take Away Your Fears,
And Guide Your Understanding...
I Will Constantly Assure You,
That I Will Always Be Here
Right Beside You;
And Give You A Warm Embrace,
So You Know I Care;
I Will Sit Next To You
And Tell You, You Are Wonderful,
And For All The Things You Do
You Are Incredible.
I Will Comfort You;
I Am Your Angel Through The Night;
I Will Make Sure You Are Happy,
And Everything Is Just Right.

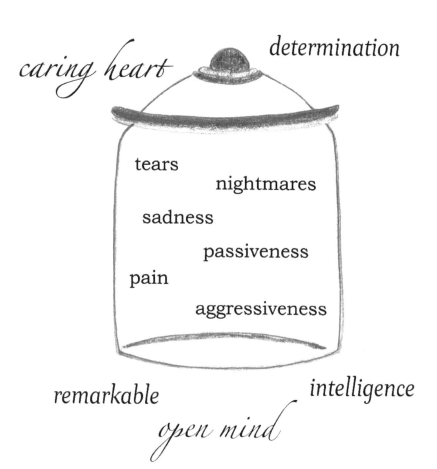

caring heart

determination

tears

nightmares

sadness

passiveness

pain

aggressiveness

remarkable

intelligence

open mind

Say No More

Your smile always hid your pain,
and laughter concealed your tears;
your busyness camouflaged the sadness,
you've been struggling with for years;
your passiveness made you cry,
and your aggressiveness made others weep;
the nightmares inhibit your ability,
of getting enough sleep.

Your determination has helped you live,
and your intelligence guided your way;
your caring heart, and open mind,
are the reasons your friends stay;
your desire to heal yourself,
from the pain from before;
is one of your most remarkable qualities...
and I need not say more!

Remembering Myself

I remember myself,
the things I enjoy;
like drawing pictures,
and playing with toys;
I enjoy taking walks,
and writing under moon's light;
I enjoy having picnics,
really late at night;
I enjoy smelling flowers,
and admiring the trees;
I enjoy going hiking,
and sitting by streams;
I enjoy warm weather,
and weather that is cold;
I enjoy making sand-castles,
and angels in snow;
I enjoy piano music,
to listen and to play;
I enjoying remembering myself,
each night and day!

caring

mindful

SALUTARY

considerate

compassionate

ASSIDUOUS

PEACEFUL

available

intelligent

DEDICATED

HEALING

Worthy

Who I Am

A caring person,
with a desire to help heal;
A mindful person,
who knows how you feel;
A salutary person,
with a hand to lend;
A considerate person,
always there to fend;
A compassionate person,
who's not afraid of tears;
An assiduous person,
who's not just 'here;'
A peaceful person,
with a calming tone;
An available person,
late night on the phone;
An intelligent person,
with lots yet to learn;
A dedicated person,
who's here with concern;
A healing person,
because I can;
A worthy person,
is Who I Am!

Zeal!

I can't believe the happiness,
I'm feeling in my life;
I couldn't ask for more,
what I have will suffice!
I can't believe the contentment,
that I finally feel;
this is my happiness, and my contentment;
I've never felt so real!
I can't believe the laughter,
that comes from out of me;
I am now really laughing
it, before, was make-believe!
Can you imagine? It's me smiling?
Take a look at my teeth!
It's hard to accept me smiling,
when before I'd only weep.
This is the new me,
and all the feelings that I feel;
can be summed up into one word...

Zeal!

A Reason To Believe

There's an important reason to believe;
that reason is me.

There's a primary reason to survive;
that reason is me.

There's a significant reason to succeed;
that reason is me.

There's an essential reason to smile;
that reason is me.

There's a critical reason to live;
that reason is me.

There's an important reason to **believe** ...
A primary reason to **survive** ...
There's a significant reason to **succeed** ...
An essential reason to **smile** ...
There's a critical reason to live ...

That reason is me.

That Reason Is Me.

THAT REASON IS ME.

But I have to believe!

My World

I am a believer,
so I will believe;
I will believe in a world
enjoyable for me.

I will fill it with happiness,
and stock it with cheer;
there will be piano music
that I will always hear.

There will only be those,
who solely express love;
my world will be bright
with walking stars above.

I will have green valleys,
and rivers and streams;
everything will be great
just because I believe!

The Trouble With Secrets?

You may never heal;
no one knows what's going on,
how you really feel;
you can easily put on a smile,
and act as if nothing is wrong;
you can put on a convincing act,
but only for so long.
The trouble with secrets?
They tear you apart;
you have to discuss your secrets,
now, to have a clear heart.

No more secrets

PERIOD

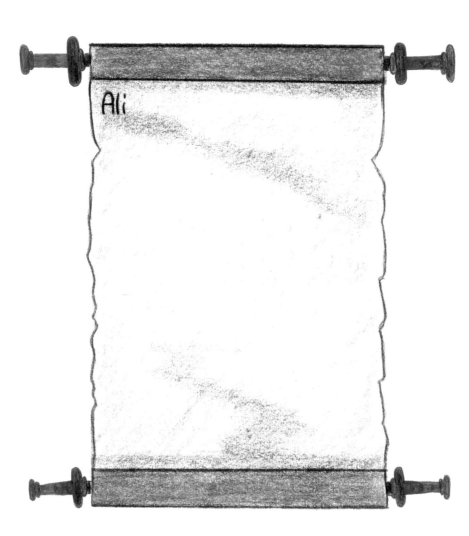

Join Me In Healing

Do you want to experience,
the best times of your life?
Do you want to be content?
Truly happy? Without strife?
Do you want to smile,
from the inside out?
Do you want to go through life,
with happiness, and hope?
Do you want to heal yourself,
from issues in your past?
Then join me in healing,
so happiness will last.

I Am A Survivor!

I Am A Survivor!
Survivor Is Me!
I Believe In Myself!
In Me, I Believe!
I Am Extraordinary!
Extraordinary I Am!
I Can Do Anything!
Because Survivor ...
I Am!

Help Me To Believe

Get on my side,
not on my case;
speak gently to me,
don't yell in my face;
tell me good things I'm doing,
with the changes I have made;
don't constantly tell me,
how I've misbehaved;
tell me how proud you are,
of the things I do well;
comment when things I say,
make your heart swell;
tell me how great I am,
it helps me to succeed;
tell me only positive things,
that will help me to believe.

Relax!

Take your time,
and think things through;
plan very carefully,
what you want to do;
there's no need to rush,
your life will be here;
tranquility of mind,
you should not fear.

Take your time,
and don't let yourself down,
because if you hasten like this,
no satisfaction will be found;
take time out,
and enjoy your life;
take the day off,
and don't think twice.

Keep on your pajamas,
and put your feet up;
sip on your favorite drink,
from your favorite cup;
take a bath,
and read from a great book; then
get out your most favorite recipes;
the most delicious things to cook.

Relax the day away,
for you owe it to you;
you deserve some ease today,
for all the work you do.

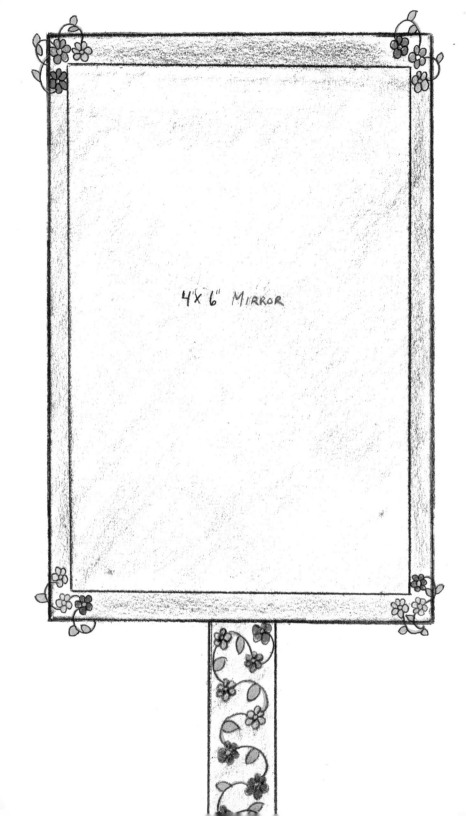

4'x 6" MIRROR

All You Really Need!

You say you need something
you can believe in?

I'm going to give you hints
on where to begin:

First, stand in front of a mirror ...
(a full length if you can;)

Second, say, 'Gee I'm wonderful!'
Again, and again!

Third, just admire yourself,
and the greatness that is you ...

Fourth, close your eyes,
and think of the good that you do ...

the **Fifth** thing for you to do
is open your eyes wide;

Sixth, give yourself a smile,
and say, 'I'm glad to be alive!'

You say you need something
in which to believe?

The image looking back at you
is all you really need!

Other Publications

Book I: **Sporadic Memories**: 'A novel about a lifestyle that needs to be read about.'

Books II & III: **Because of Grandfather** and **Because of Grandmother**: 'Both an elaboration on the lifestyle lived in Sporadic Memories through the eyes of the Grandson and Granddaughter.'

CPSIA information can be obtained
at www.ICGtesting.com
Printed in the USA
LVHW02n2157180218
567075LV00001B/1/P